This Book Belongs to:

WHEN IN DOUBT

Writer - Illustrator:

Christiana Forbes

Copyright © CHRISTIANA Forbes 2024

All rights reserved. No part of this book may be reproduced or transmitted in any form or by any means, electronic or mechanical, including photocopying, recording, or by any information storage and retrieval system, without permission in writing from the copyright owner.

This is a work of fiction. Names, characters, places, and incidents are either the product of the author's imagination or are used fictitiously. Any resemblance to actual persons, living or dead, business establishments, events, or locales is entirely coincidental.

For permissions or inquiries, contact:
Christiana Forbes
khiara.christiana@gmail.com

Cover Illustration by Christiana Forbes

First Edition: January, 2024

I dedicate this book to my daughter Ariana,
The brightest star in my sky.
May these pages reflect the warmth of your light,
Just as you bring warmth to my life.

...but my love for you never fades.

Voices that tell you that you're not enough...

...Block out doubt's noisy sound, you're strong, and that strength is so profound!

Your lovely smile,
a treasure so rare,
bringing warmth and love,
beyond compare...

Few words about the writer

Born on a crispy winter day in 1990, Christiana's journey through life has been a tale of resilience, creativity, and a love for the written word. From a young age, books became her refuge, opening doorways to magical realms where imagination knew no bounds.

As the years passed, she decided to channel her creativity into a formal education, pursuing a degree in Applied Multimedia. This journey not only honed her artistic skills but also ignited a flame within her to bring stories to life through a vibrant blend of visuals and words.

Since childhood, Christiana faced the challenges of a congenital heart disease with unwavering courage. In the midst of her personal battles, a four-legged companion named Khiara entered Christiana's life—a beagle with soulful eyes and a heart as resilient as her own. Khiara became not only a loyal friend but the muse for Christiana's first-ever story.

When Christiana delved into the realms of motherhood, her creativity took on new dimensions. The arrival of her two children brought joy and inspiration, infusing her stories with the magic of familial bonds and the simple wonders of childhood.

However, the story of Christiana Forbes is not just about conquering the challenges of health or weaving tales of wonder; it's a celebration of embracing vulnerability and turning it into a source of strength.

Made in the USA
Coppell, TX
14 February 2024